Sharks

LEVEL **3** READER

READING LEVEL
GRADES 2 TO 4

Written by Dalton Prescott
Illustrated by Matthew Jeffirs

Franklin, Tennessee 37068-2068   1-866-418-2572
dalmatianpress.com

The Ultimate Predator

Sharks are fish. Like other fish, they live in the water, have fins, breathe with gills, and most are cold blooded. Unlike other fish, the skeleton of a shark is made of cartilage (like the cartilage in your ear) instead of bone.

Shark Bites
A shark's mouth can have up to six rows of teeth. When one tooth falls out, another takes its place, usually about every two weeks.

Sharks are considered to be ultimate predators,
not only because of their power, speed, and sharp teeth,
but because they have super senses. Sharks have
excellent noses for smelling, eyes that can see well
underwater, ears that pick up tiny sounds, and spots
all over their bodies that allow them to "taste" the
water. Sharks also have extra senses that help them
feel vibrations, pressure waves,
and electrical charges.

Shark Bites
Two-thirds of a shark's
brain is dedicated to smell.
A shark can detect a
single drop of blood in
an Olympic-sized pool.

Mako Shark

Sharks come in many colors
and sizes—from the size of a
banana to over 40 feet!

The mako shark lives in tropical and temperate waters.
It can reach speeds of 25 mph and leap out of the water!
Mako sharks and blue sharks are some of the fastest fish
in any ocean. The mako shark is a fierce predator. It hunts
schooling fish like tuna, mackerel, and swordfish.

Shark Bites
Shark jaws are not connected
to the skull, so the jaws can be
unhinged to open very wide
for eating.

Whitetip Reef Shark

The whitetip reef shark is an easygoing shark named for the white tip on its dorsal (back) fin. It can grow to seven feet long. The whitetip reef shark is the shark most often seen by divers in tropical reefs.

Shark Bites
There are more than 350 kinds of sharks. Most live in warm seas.

Lanternshark

The lanternshark is a glow-in-the-dark fish that lives in the Atlantic and Pacific oceans. It lives deep on the sandy bottom where there is little light. The lanternshark has special organs on its side and belly that produce a greenish light. This light helps it find a mate and startle predators.

Shark Bites
Most sharks give birth to live young, but some "lay" eggs in sacs that hatch later.

Lemon Shark

The lemon shark gets its name from the yellowish brown color on its back and sides. This coloring helps the lemon shark blend in with the sand on the ocean floor. These aggressive sharks live along the southeastern coast of the United States. Lemon sharks eat bony fish, shrimp, crabs, and other small sharks. They can grow to be 10 feet long!

Shark Bites
A lemon shark can learn faster than a cat or a rabbit and can be trained to navigate a maze faster than a rat!

Great White Shark

The white shark, known as the great white, is named for its white belly. This is the most recognized, feared, and admired of all sharks. With its powerful jaws and hundreds of sharp teeth, this deadly predator eats large animals, like sea turtles, sea lions, and seals. It is fearless and has even been known to attack boats!

The great white can grow to more than 20 feet long—the size of a bus! (The females are bigger than the males.) They swim through the ocean at speeds of 15 mph.

Great whites usually attack from below, surprising their victims. They can even leap out of the water completely to lunge at their prey! They take a bite, then move away and wait. Once their prey has lost blood, it is much easier to finish off.

Shark Bites
When a great white attacks, its eyeballs roll back into its head to protect them from injury.

Shark Bites
Other names for the great white are white pointer and white death.

Shark Bites
A pregnant great white can carry as many as 12 babies in her belly. At birth, a pup can weigh up to 60 pounds!

Blacktip Reef Shark

The blacktip reef shark—whose fins are tipped with black markings—travels in groups. Up to seven feet long, the blacktip prefers swimming around coral reefs and shallow lagoons. It is mainly a fish eater, though it will also eat squid, octopuses, and shrimp.

Like other sharks, the blacktip has tiny pores on its head that are deep and full of jelly. These pores connect to nerves that allow a shark to sense the faint electrical pulses of living things.

Shark Bites

Each year, thousands of sharks get tangled in fishing nets and die. Many sharks are no threat to humans.

Tiger Shark

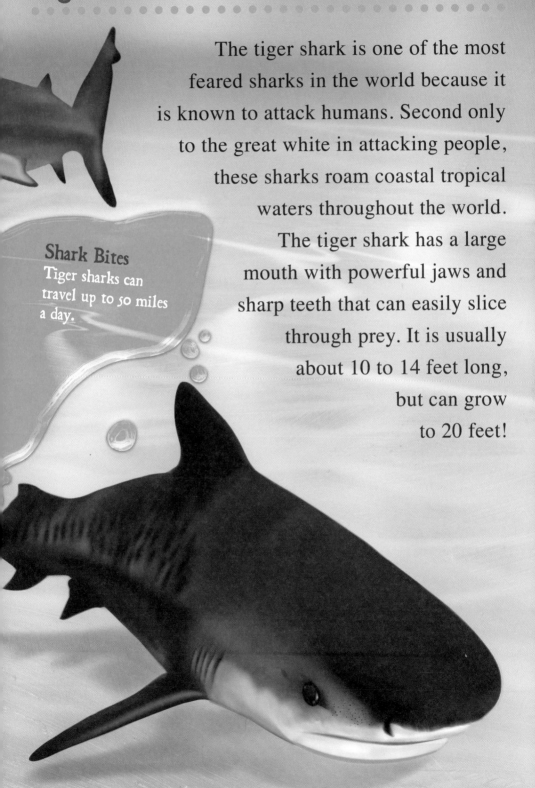

The tiger shark is one of the most feared sharks in the world because it is known to attack humans. Second only to the great white in attacking people, these sharks roam coastal tropical waters throughout the world. The tiger shark has a large mouth with powerful jaws and sharp teeth that can easily slice through prey. It is usually about 10 to 14 feet long, but can grow to 20 feet!

Shark Bites
Tiger sharks can travel up to 50 miles a day.

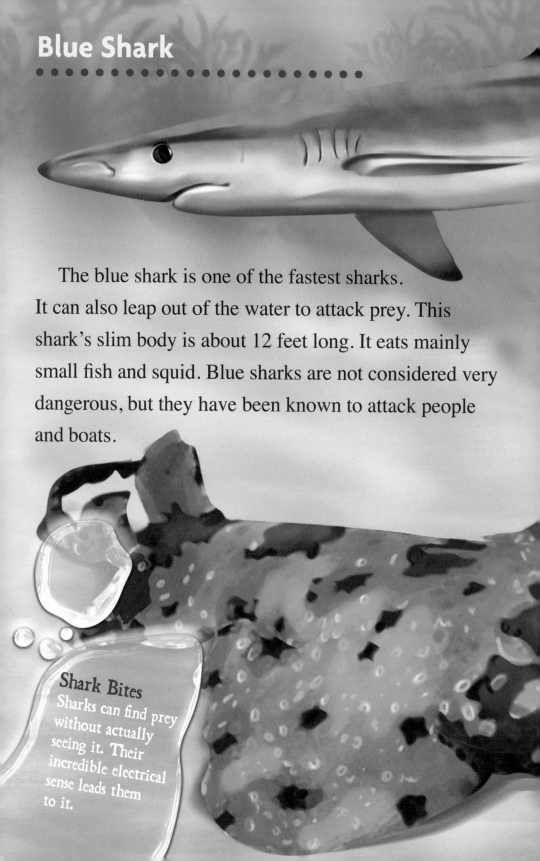

Blue Shark

The blue shark is one of the fastest sharks. It can also leap out of the water to attack prey. This shark's slim body is about 12 feet long. It eats mainly small fish and squid. Blue sharks are not considered very dangerous, but they have been known to attack people and boats.

Shark Bites
Sharks can find prey without actually seeing it. Their incredible electrical sense leads them to it.

Wobbegong Shark

The wobbegong shark is a type of carpet shark that lives in the Australian and Pacific coral reefs. This shark gets its unique name from the Aborigines (native people in Australia). It has sharp teeth and it can grow to 9 feet long. It also has camouflaged skin that matches the pattern of coral and rocks on the sea floor. This allows the wobbegong to sneak up on small fish without being seen.

Shark Bites

Fish have smooth skin covered in scales. Sharks have rough skin covered with denticles: razor-sharp, toothlike projections.

Thresher Shark

Of all the sharks, the thresher shark has the longest tail. The upper part of its tail can be the same length as the rest of its body! The thresher uses its tail to thresh (beat) the water when it finds a school of fish. This forces the fish into a tight group and makes it easier for the shark to kill its prey.

Shark Bites
Sharks can hear more than 800 feet away and see for a distance of about 50 feet.

Hammerhead Shark

The hammerhead shark is considered dangerous because of its large size and predatory nature. The hammerhead can grow to a size of 20 feet long and weigh up to 1,000 pounds! Because of the shape of its head, this shark's eyes and nostrils are far apart. This expands its range of senses. Hammerheads usually travel in schools (packs)—sometimes in groups of 60 or more!

Shark Bites

The hammerhead shark gets stung while eating stingrays, its favorite food. Scientists believe that hammerheads may have natural immunity to the stings.

Silky Shark

The silky shark is named for its smooth
skin. It has a large, slender body and a
rounded snout. It is usually found in
the open ocean and can migrate great
distances. The silky is sometimes
considered dangerous because it
is large, fast, and aggressive,
but it is more likely to be threatened
by man than be a threat to man.

Shark Bites
Some sharks can bite
through thick steel!
And some can go
months without eating.

Pygmy Shark

The pygmy shark, one of the smallest known sharks, is only about 8 inches long! This shark lives deep in the sea by day, but moves close to the surface at night to hunt for squid, shrimp, and lanternfish.

Shark Bites

Sharks are related to manta rays and stingrays, which also have cartilage instead of bone.

Whale Shark

Don't let its name and size fool you—the whale shark it not a whale. It is the world's biggest shark and the world's biggest fish, too! It can grow to 40 feet long and weigh up to 20 tons! Whale sharks lumber along slowly, eating plankton and tiny fish. These gentle giants can live for over 100 years!

Shark Bites
The whale shark is the world's largest fish but eats some of the smallest living things in the ocean.

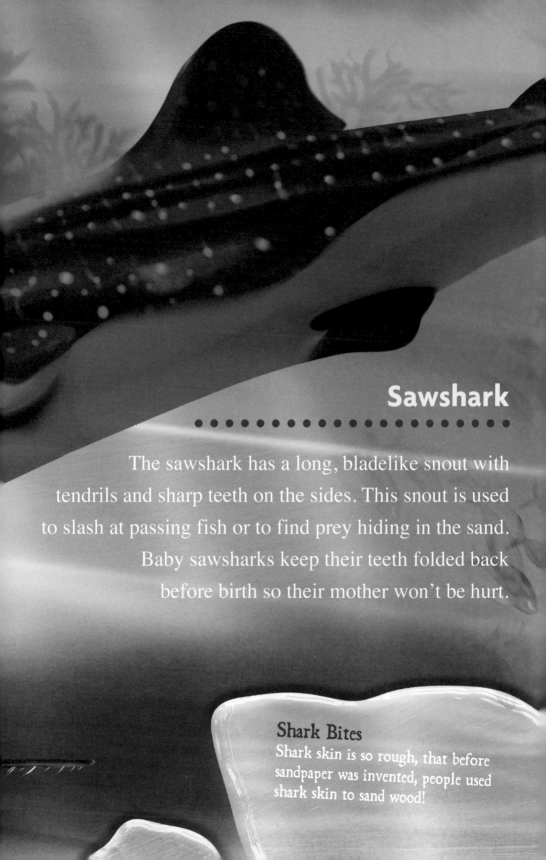

Sawshark

The sawshark has a long, bladelike snout with tendrils and sharp teeth on the sides. This snout is used to slash at passing fish or to find prey hiding in the sand. Baby sawsharks keep their teeth folded back before birth so their mother won't be hurt.

Shark Bites
Shark skin is so rough, that before sandpaper was invented, people used shark skin to sand wood!

Conservation

Shark Bites
A person is more likely to drown in the ocean or be killed by hornets, wasps, or bees than die from a shark attack.

Sharks may be the top predators in the ocean, but they are in danger of extinction at the hands of humans. Fishing, hunting, and habitat destruction are causing a sharp decline in the population of sharks in our waters. Sharks are hunted for sport and trophies, as well as for food and materials. Sharks are also killed when they get caught in nets used for fishing or for protecting beaches.

Some sharks are dangerous to humans and have been known to attack. The sharks that are considered to be most dangerous to humans are the great white, tiger, and bull sharks. Some scientists think that sharks have mistaken humans for other large prey, like seals or sea lions. Most often, shark attacks happen when humans have ventured too far into shark territory or are hunting sharks. Most shark bites are the result of a shark's curiosity—and are not fatal. Humans are not on the menu!

Shark Bites
On average, sharks kill 10 people each year. Humans kill millions of sharks each year.

Myths and Mysteries

There are almost as many shark myths and mysteries as there are species. Are all sharks vicious killers? Will they eat almost anything? And do all sharks live in the ocean?

Shark can see in the dark. *True.* **They have excellent night vision and are about 10 times more sensitive to light than humans.**

Sharks will eat anything. *False.* Some do eat some garbage, but sharks prefer fish, crabs, squid, stingrays, other sharks, and plankton. One of their least favorite foods is human beings.

Sharks have an endless supply of teeth. *True.* Sharks continuously produce teeth, which are loosely attached to their jaws.

All sharks are man-eaters. *False.* Most are too small to kill humans, and some, like the giant whale shark, eat only plankton, krill, or small fish. Others live in the deep sea far away from people.

Punching a shark in the nose is a great defense. *False.* A shark's nose is sensitive, but its skin is thick. Trying to punch anything through water is also difficult.

Sharks can find prey without seeing or smelling them. *True.* Sharks have an incredible electrical sense that leads them to prey hidden in muddy waters or buried in the sea floor. The sound of a struggling fish also attracts sharks.

Sharks are smart. *True.* Sharks have large brains and can be quite intelligent.

Dolphins can deter sharks from attacking. *Possibly.* When researchers threw a seal-shaped lure into the shark-infested waters of South Africa recently, they found that the sharks attacked fast. But when a fake dolphin was dropped into the water, the sharks stayed back.

Jaws of Life

Shark Bites
Sharks keep our oceans healthy by feeding on a wide variety of species that have no other predators.

Sharks play an important role in Earth's ecosystem by preying on the weak and sick. Without sharks, the oceans would suffer. These great predators need our protection—and respect.